# A bee's guide to Garden Flowers

## Gloria Morgan

## Illustrated by Victoria White

*Happy Reading!*
*Gloria Morgan*

An environmentally friendly book printed and bound in England by www.printondemand-worldwide.com

**Mixed Sources**
Product group from well-managed
forests, and other controlled sources

**FSC**
www.fsc.org  Cert no. TT-COC-002641
© 1996 Forest Stewardship Council

**PEFC**
PEFC/16-33-415

**PEFC Certified**
This product is
from sustainably
managed forests
and controlled
sources
www.pefc.org

This book is made entirely of chain-of-custody materials

Dionaea Muscipula

# A few flowery words from the author

Many of the plants pictured in this book started life as seedlings on my kitchen window sill. I love flowers and flower designs. They make my house beautiful inside as well as outside.

The picture of the insect-eating plant 'Dionaea Muscipula' that upset the bee in the first place appears on a plate on the dresser in my kitchen.

I avoid serving a meal on it to guests. It could be shocking to see such a violent scene emerging as you get to the end of your dinner.

The whole thing was my fault for leaving the back door open. You could say the bee shouldn't have flown in, but you know what they're like. I've now bought a bead curtain for summer days.

There are many placid, good-tempered bees buzzing round my garden, along with butterflies, moths, ladybirds and dragonflies. I love them all.

*Gloria Morgan*

# The Bee's Story

I'm a bee.
Right? A bee. That's me.
I'm gonna guide you round
       the flower bedz
Like the title sez.
Only there's one thing, before we go,
You should know.
I 'ate flars.
This is becars
I seen a picture of a bee being
       eaten by a plant.
I fink it was my aunt.
Due to that atrocity
I vowed to become a secret killer bee.
Made me so mad. I fought
In future, I'm gonna make your sort
Pay for what occurred.
Didn't try it on wiv a bird
Or a cat,
Or anyfing as big as that.
No it was a humble
Little bee, a bumble
Bee, as a matter of fact.

Oi - I've noticed you react
To the way I e-nun-ci-ate.
Well, listen, mate
If what you 'ad to do all day wuz
Flap your wings like mad until you buzz
You wouldn't ave the bref
Lef'
To talk in normal phrases.
It amazes
Me what confusion it causes
Because of where I put my pauses.
I find it perfectly clear.
So - listen 'ere.
All these plants will grow to order
In any garden border.
Don't make me explain no more.
Let's get on wiv this guided tour
Wivout any more talk.
Lessee some blossom 'n'
       branches 'n' stalk.
I'm a bee, see.
Lucky I'm talking to you at all,
       if you ask me ...

**A**

stands for **Arch**

and
Aster and
Anthemis

and Alium

Berberis Berries in autumn

stands for

# Berberis

Bridal Wreath ('Foam of May') &
Balm - lemon scented

Bacopa - white & mauve

**C stands for Clematis**

and Coreopsis

and Cleome

and Crocosmia

and don't forget the dog ...

and Delphinium

stands for
Dahlia

Eremurus - 'the fox- tail lily'

Endymion - the bluebell

and Echinops - Globe Thistle

and Erysimum - perpetual wallflower

E stands for
**Eremurus**

and Fritillaria

and Foxglove

stands for
Fuchsia

and Forget-me-not and Forsythia

G stands for Geranium

and Gazania

and Gaura

Geranium 'Vancouver Centenniel'
and Geranium 'Raiko'

# H stands for Helenium

Helianthus Annuus - sunflower, and Hollyhock

and Hosta

Hesperis Metronalis (sweet rocket)

stands for **Iris**

and **Ipomoea**

**J** stands for **Japanese Maple**

Tree in flower, before the leaves open

'Red Hot Poker'

**K** stands for **Kniphofia**

and Lilac

and Lupin

stands for
Leucanthemum

and Lonicera - Honeysuckle

M stands
for
Marigold

Michaelmas Daisy

Malus in fruit

Mint

Malus in flower

**N** stands
for
# Nasturtium

and Narcissus

Nicotiana -
sweet-scented
'Tobacco plant'

**O** stands for

# Oriental
# Poppy

### with Campanula

Cynoglossum nervosum 'Hound's tongue'

Perpetual Sweet Pea 'Lathyrus'

Q stands for the Quivering Plant

P stands for Peony

# **R** stands for Roses

Solidago - Golden rod

Sedum

Saxifraga - 'London Pride'

'The Blue Potato Bush'

Scarlet Salvia

**S** stands for

Solanum

**T** stands for

# Tulips

and Tagetes

and Thunbergeria

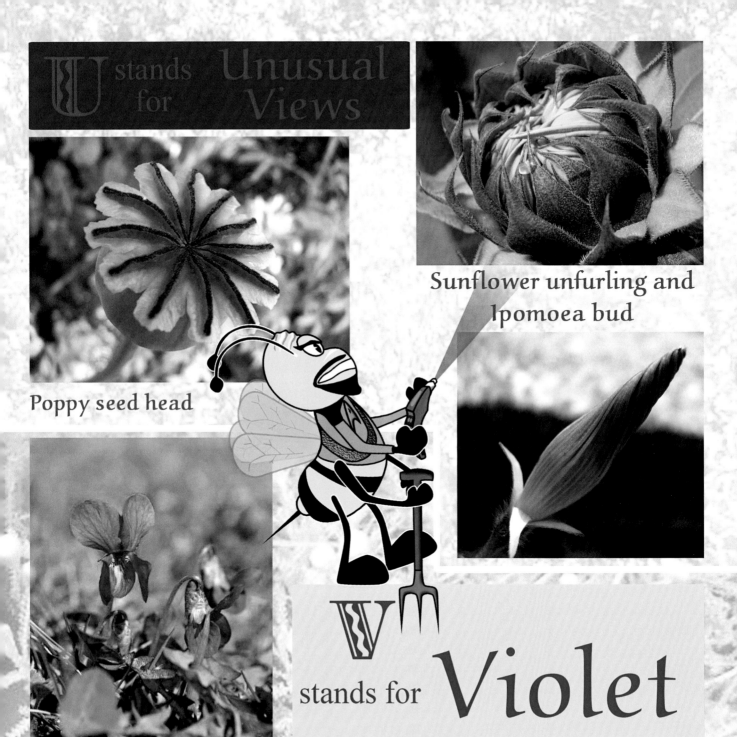

**U** stands for **Unusual Views**

Poppy seed head

Sunflower unfurling and Ipomoea bud

**V** stands for **Violet**

**W** stands for
# Water Lily

and Weigela

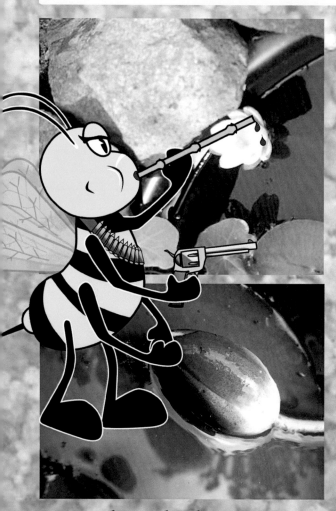

Bud and Blossom

**X** stands for
## Xeranthemum

'Everlasting' flower

Xmas rose
– Helleborus Niger

or Achillea Millefolium

Z
stands for
Zinnia

Y
stands for
Yarrow

# The Bee's Postscript

Hang on a mo.
Some Joe
Just told me those plants are called Venus's FLY traps
So p'rhaps
The one that I saw wasn't eating a bee, after all.
In that case, it would fall
To me to apologise and repent
Of all the mayhem on which I was intent.
But I must say,
If you should encounter a killer fly one day,
Out gunning for every flar of which it 'ears
Becars a plant ate a relative of theirs,
Don't say you weren't warned by me -
The now EX-secret killer bee!

# *Thanks*

All the flower photographs you have enjoyed in this book were taken in my garden by myself, Victoria White and Rachel Boden, to whom many thanks for their stunning images.

Victoria White drew and illustrated the bee and made it fly with attitude through the alphabet. Victoria was also responsible for the design and layout of the pages.

In creating my garden I owe much gratitude to Kathryn Goodwin for sharing her immense knowledge of plants and doing a lot of digging.

The flowery tableware in my kitchen is Portmeirion 'The Botanic Garden'™.

Like the Bee says - "plants will grow to order in any garden border", so what are you waiting for? Get a few seeds, a bag of compost and some little pots and away you go! Bees could soon be buzzing in your very own flower garden.

# How my garden began to grow

A few years ago I spent my summer holidays in France. While I was there I visited Monet's Garden at Giverny, north of Paris, and fell in love.

When I got home I looked at my boring garden and my heart sank, This just wouldn't do any more. There was nothing for it but to start again and create my own mini-Monet.

By the autumn I had a plan. The lawn would go and be replaced by flower beds filled with the same plants that grow in Monet's Garden.

Before the turn of the year the layout of the beds was marked out on the grass and shortly after Christmas the digging began. A January snow fall helped to break up the newly turned ground. In February the architecture of the garden was put in place.

In March, seeds for annuals were sown in pots to raise on my window sill and holes were dug for the climbing roses. April saw the beds planted out with perennials, leaving plenty of room for them to fill out as they grow. By May it began to look like a real garden. In June things were improved by the addition of gravel to the paths and the first of the roses in bloom.

In July, one year on, mini-Monet had come to life, bringing rewards of all that effort.

### Gloria Morgan